MW01690601

The Road to Good Friendship

First Edition: November 1999

Supervised by:
ABDUL MALIK MUJAHID

Head Office:

DARUSSALAM
P.O. Box 22743, Riyadh 11416, Kingdom of Saudi Arabia
Tel: 00966-1-403 3962/404 3432 Fax: 00966-1-402 1659
E-mail: darussalam@naseej.com.sa

Branches:

DARUSSALAM
50, Lower Mall, Lahore, Pakistan. Tel: 0092-42-724 0024/723 2400
Fax: 0092-42-735 4072

DARUSSALAM PUBLICATIONS

P.O. Box. 79194, Houston, TX 77279, USA. Tel: 001-713-722 0419
Fax: 001-713-722 0431
E-mail: sales@dar-us-salam.com **Website:** www.dar-us-salam.com

DARUSSALAM

572-Atlantic Ave, Brooklyn, New York 11217, USA. Tel: 001-718-625 5925

AL-HIDAÂYAH PUBLISHING & DISTRIBUTION

522 Coventry Road, Birmingham, B10 OUN, UK. Tel: 0044-121-753 1889
Fax: 0044-121-753 2422

رفقـــاء طريـــق

The Road to Good Friendship

By

Abdul Malik bin Muhammad Ibn Abdur Rahman Al-Qasim

Translated by

Jalal Abualrub

Published by

DARUSSALAM

Publishers and Distributors

Riyadh, Saudi Arabia

بسم الله الرحمن الرحيم

In the Name of Allâh
the Most Gracious, the Most Merciful.

"Muhammad ﷺ is the Messenger of Allâh. And those who are with him are severe against disbelievers, and merciful among themselves. You see them bowing and falling down prostrate (in prayer), seeking Bounty from Allâh and (His) Good Pleasure. The mark of them (i.e., of their Faith) is on their faces (foreheads) from the traces of prostration (during prayers). This is their description in the Taurât (Torah). But their description in the Injeel (Gospel) is like a (sown) seed which sends forth its shoot, then makes it strong, and becomes thick and it stands straight on its stem, delighting the sowers, that He may enrage the disbelievers with them. Allâh has promised those among them who believe and do righteous good deeds, forgiveness and a mighty reward (i.e., Paradise)." (48:29)

Publishers Note

All the praises and thanks are due to Allâh, the *Rubb* of the worlds, and may Allâh exalt the mention of the Prophet Muhammad, the chosen, the trustworthy, and the mention of his Household and all of his Companions.

The Road to Good Friendship is very enlightening booklet by Abdul-Malik Al-Qasim, a renowned religion scholar and an expert of Arabic language.

Islam is the message of welfare. There are obligatory rights and duties among the relatives, neighbors, working-partners and friends in Islam and these all human rights have described in the Book of Allah and *Ahadith* (sayings of the Prophet ﷺ). In addition, our *Salaf* have many good examples not only for the Muslim society but also for the other religion peoples. In this book, the author has collected good examples and advices of the *Salaf* that will encourage the readers for a good friendship.

In view of its importance, Darussalam has rendered this booklet into the English language with prior permission from the author. Brother Jalal Abualrub accepted the task of translation, and performed it very well.

Finally, I am grateful to all brothers who have contributed in bringing about this valuable book. May Allâh accept our sincere efforts regarding the propagation of His religion throughout the world, and bestow on us His blessings to fulfill our resolution in this regard — *Âmin*!

Abdul Malik Mujahid
General Manager

Introduction

All thanks and praises are due to Allâh, Lord of all that exists, and may Allâh's peace and blessings be on Muhammad, the most honorable Messenger and Prophet.

Islam is the religion of purity, brotherhood, kindness and affection, as is evident by the many *Âyât* in the Book of Allâh the Exalted, and the many *Ahadith* in the *Sunnah* of His Messenger that legislate these types of honorable conduct that Islam brought. In this book, I collected several examples of stories and tales of good company and friendship by our *Salaf*,[1] because of the importance of being in good company and associating with righteous people, especially in the present time.

'*The Road to Good Friendship*' is a small but beneficial booklet.

I ask Allâh the Exalted to help us fulfill the rights and obligations of sincere brotherhood and to gather us and our loved ones as righteous companions under the shade of His Throne.

Abdul Malik ibn Muhammad
Ibn Abdul Rahman Al-Qasim

---

1 The *Salaf* are the Companions, the *Tabi'in* (second generation of Companions), and the third generation of Islam, are the best people as the Prophet ﷺ described them.

Who is Friend?

In the life of the world, while travelling through the various stages of life, man needs good friends, associates and companions to provide comfort and righteous company on the road and throughout the journey that every one must and shall take and go on. One's company and friends he or she associates with are a source of help and relief when disasters strike, feeling elated when one is elated and sad when one is sad, if they are true and righteous friends whom Allâh has endowed with a religious nature, as well as, good behavior and exalted conduct. This company is, and must be, of the righteous, sincere, advising, good mannered, truthful and religious Muslim.

There is no doubt that good conduct produces the fruits of affection, kindness and comfort, and the better one's conduct becomes, the tastier and sweeter the fruit becomes. Allâh has often mentioned favorably ties of affection and closeness between companions, providing that their companionship is built on the basis of piety, Islamic religion and love of Allâh. Furthermore, Allâh has reminded Prophet Muhammad ﷺ and the believers of His great Bounty and Favor that:

﴿ لَوْ أَنفَقْتَ مَا فِي ٱلْأَرْضِ جَمِيعًا مَّآ أَلَّفْتَ بَيْنَ قُلُوبِهِمْ وَلَٰكِنَّ ٱللَّهَ أَلَّفَ بَيْنَهُمْ ﴾ [الأنفال : ٦٣]

"If you (Muhammad ﷺ) had spent all that is in the earth, you could not have united their hearts, but Allâh has united them." (8:63)

Allâh has also admonished and outlawed division:

﴿ وَٱعْتَصِمُوا۟ بِحَبْلِ ٱللَّهِ جَمِيعًا وَلَا تَفَرَّقُوا۟ ۚ وَٱذْكُرُوا۟ نِعْمَتَ ٱللَّهِ عَلَيْكُمْ إِذْ كُنتُمْ أَعْدَآءً فَأَلَّفَ بَيْنَ قُلُوبِكُمْ فَأَصْبَحْتُم بِنِعْمَتِهِۦٓ إِخْوَٰنًا وَكُنتُمْ عَلَىٰ شَفَا حُفْرَةٍ مِّنَ

﴿ٱلنَّارِ فَأَنقَذَكُم مِّنْهَا كَذَٰلِكَ يُبَيِّنُ ٱللَّهُ لَكُمْ ءَايَٰتِهِۦ لَعَلَّكُمْ تَهْتَدُونَ﴾
[آل عمران: ١٠٣]

"And hold fast, all of you together, to the Rope of Allâh (i.e., this Qur'ân), and be not divided among yourselves, and remember Allâh's Favour on you, for you were enemies one to another but He joined your hearts together, so that, by His Grace, you became brethren (in Islâmic Faith); and you were on the brink of a pit of Fire, and He saved you from it. Thus Allâh makes His *Ayât* clear to you, that you may be guided." (3:103)

Further, the Messenger of Allâh ﷺ said:

«إنَّ أقرَبَكم مِنِّي مَجْلسًا أحاسِنُكم أَخْلاقًا المُوَطَّئُون أَكْنافًا، الَّذين يَألفُون ويُؤْلَفُون».

"Verily, those among you who will have the closest seats to me (on the Day of Resurrection) are they who have the best conduct, who are humble, who easily get along and are easy to get along with. (*At-Tabarani*)"[1]

Having feelings of love for Allâh's sake and brotherly ties in the religions are two of the best acts of obedience and worship. Furthermore, there are conditions and guidelines that qualify Muslims to be among those who love each other for Allâh's sake, and rights to fulfill in this regard that will purify brotherhood from all impurities and evil plots of Satan, in addition to, drawing closer to Allâh, the Exalted. Moreover, by preserving these rights and obligations, one will earn the highest grades and ranks (with Allâh).[2]

---

1 *Al-Ihyâ'*, vol. 2, p. 171

2 *Al-Ihyâ'*, vol. 2, p. 171

Know that not everyone is suitable to be a friend. Abu Hurairah رضى الله عنه narrated that the Messenger of Allâh ﷺ said:

«الرَّجُلُ على دِينِ خَلِيـلِهِ فَلْينظُرْ أَحَدكُم من يُخالِلُ».

"Man is on the religion of his companion, so let one of you choose whom to befriend."(*Ahmad*, *Abu Dâwud* and *At-Tirmidhi*, *An-Nawawi* rendered this *Hadith* authentic)

There are signs, qualities and indications that help one distinguish and choose whom to befriend and associate with according to what one desires from friendship or companionship.

There are religious and material gains to look for in any friendship or association. Material gains include earning money, fame or just friendship and companionship. Religious gains from friendship include learning religious knowledge and imitating righteous actions and statements, so that one might be helped to repel all types of impurity that might attack the heart and hinder from performing the acts of worship.

Therefore, dear Muslim, choose a friend or a companion who is wise, good mannered and righteous, who is neither a sinner, innovator in the religion or fond of this life.[1]

Allâh has praised good company and made it one of the reasons behind earning Paradise. The Messenger of Allâh ﷺ said:

«إن اللهَ تَعَالى يَقولُ يومَ القِيامَة: أين المُتَحابُّون بِجَلالي، اليَوْمَ أُظِلُّهمْ في ظِلِّي يومَ لا ظِلَّ إلا ظِلِّي».

---

[1] *Al-Ihyâ'*, vol. 2, p. 186

"Allâh the Exalted will declare on the Day of Resurrection: 'Where are those who loved each other for the sake of My Grace? This Day, I shall shade them under My Shade, when there is only My Shade.'" (*Muslim*)

In addition, the Messenger of Allâh ﷺ said:

«سَبْعةٌ يُظِلُّهم اللهُ في ظِلِّهِ يَوْمَ لَا ظلَّ إلَّا ظِلُّه: إمامٌ عادلٌ، وشابٌّ نَشَأَ فِي طَاعةِ الله، ورَجُلٌ قلبُه مُتَعَلِّق بالمَسْجِدِ إذَا خَرَجَ منه حَتَّى يَعودَ إليه، وَرَجُلان تحابَّا في الله اجْتَمَعا عَلىٰ ذٰلك وتَفَرَّقا عليه...».

"Allâh will give shade to seven, on the Day when there will be no shade but His. (These seven persons are): 1. A just ruler; 2. A youth who has brought up in the worship of Allâh (i.e., worships Allâh sincerely from childhood); 3. A man whose heart is attached to the mosque (i.e., worships Allâh sincerely from childhood) from the time he leaves it until he goes back to it (for the next prayer); 4. Two persons who love each other only for Allâh's sake and they meet and part in Allâh's cause only; 5. A man who refuses the call of a charming woman of noble birth for an illegal sexual, intercourse with her and says: 'I am afraid of Allâh; 6. A person who practices charity so secretly that his left hand does not know what his right hand has given (i.e., nobody knows how much he has given in charity); and 7. A person who remembers Allâh in seclusion and his eyes become flooded with tears." (*Al-Bukhâri* and *Muslim*)

One's companion is just like the mirror, it reflects his or her image and reveals to the people one's true reality and essence. This is why it is important that each one of us uses special care to choose whomever he or she wants for friend.

Abu Sulaiman said:

> "The Prophet's statement that one follows the religion of his friend, means, befriend only he whom you are pleased with his religious conduct and honesty, for if you take such a person to be your friend, he will direct you to his religious nature and honesty. Furthermore, do not compromise in religion or risk befriending those who are unacceptable religiously or in their mannerism."[1]

Moreover, Allâh has described the condition friends will be in on the Day of Resurrection, which is the greatest and most momentous horror of all:

﴿ٱلْأَخِلَّآءُ يَوْمَئِذٍۭ بَعْضُهُمْ لِبَعْضٍ عَدُوٌّ إِلَّا ٱلْمُتَّقِينَ﴾ [الزخرف: ٦٧]

"Friends on that Day will be foes one to another except *Al-Muttaqûn* (the pious)." (43:67)

The Prophet ﷺ made an extraordinary parable with regards to righteous and evil company, when he said:

«إنَّما مَثَلُ الجَلِيس الصَّالح وجَلِيسِ السَّوء، كحَامِلِ المِسْك، ونَافِخِ الكِيرِ؛ فَحَامِلُ المِسْكِ إما أَنْ يُحذِيَك، وإما أَنْ تَبْتَاعَ منه، وإما أَنْ تَجِد منه رِيحًا طَيِّبَة. ونَافِخُ الكِير، إما أن يُحرِقَ ثيابَك، وإما أن تَجِدَ منه رِيحًا مُنْتِنَةً».

"Verily, the example of a good companion (who sits with you) in comparison with an evil one is like that of the musk seller and the blacksmith's bellows (or

---

[1] *Al-'Uzlah*, p. 510

furnace). From the first you would either get a gift of his musk's scent, buy some from him, or enjoy its good smell, while the bellows will either burn your clothes, or you give a bad, nasty smell thereof." (*Al-Bukhâri* and *Muslim* collected this authentic *Hadith*)

Also, 'Ali رضى الله عنه said:

> "Befriend righteous people, for they are a good resource to use in this and the Last Life. Have you not heard the statement of the people of the Fire:
>
> ﴿ فَمَا لَنَا مِن شَٰفِعِينَ ۝ وَلَا صَدِيقٍ حَمِيمٍ ﴾ [الشعراء: ١٠٠-١٠١]
>
> 'Now we have no intercessors. Nor a close friend (to help us).'" (26:100,101)[1]

There are duties and obligations required from friends, as 'Ata bin Maisarah stated:

> "If you do not meet for three days, check on your brethren: visit them if they are ill, help them if they are busy (i.e., help them conduct their life affairs, if you are able to do so) and remind them (of Allâh, their religious duties, performing acts of worship, and so forth) if they forget."[2]

Abu Ali Ar-Ribati said:

> "Once, I accompanied Abdullah Ar-Razi, who often took journeys to the desert, and he asked me, 'Who should lead us, you or I?' I said, 'You.' He asked, 'And you will obey?' I said, 'Yes.' So he took a bag in which he placed our provisions for the journey and carried it on his back. I asked him to let me carry it,

---

1 *Al-Ihyâ'*, 2:175

2 *Hilyatul-Auliyâ'*, vol. 5, p. 198

> but he replied, 'You said that I should lead, therefore, you should obey.' During that trip, rain fell on us one night, and he stood besides me covering me with his robe, sheltering me from the rain until it stopped. I said to myself, 'I wish I had died rather than telling him to be the leader.'"[1]

Who can compare these types of companions to the types we see in the present time?

Al-Ma'mun once said:

> "There are three types of companions: one who is as essential as food and cannot be done without. The second type is like medicine, used at some times, but not at other times. The third, is like a disease, it is always unneeded. However, one might be tested with the latter type, even though there is no comfort or delight in accompanying them."

It was said that people are just like trees and plants: some have shade but bear no fruits, and this is the parable of the type that is used in this life but is not beneficial in the Hereafter, just as shade that is soon bound to vanish and dissipate. Some trees and plants bear fruits but offer no shade, and this is the parable of the type that is useful for the Hereafter, but not for this life. Some trees and plants have shade and bear fruits (and this is the best type), and some have none bearing no benefit at all.

This is why it is essential that one chooses his friends carefully, having a stringent screening standard in this regard. One should make sure that his friends are among those who:

---

1 *Al-Ihyâ'*, vol. 2, p. 199

﴿ وَتَوَاصَوْاْ بِٱلْحَقِّ وَتَوَاصَوْاْ بِٱلصَّبْرِ ﴾ [العصر : ٣]

"...recommend one another to the truth, and recommend one another to patience." (103:3)

Who help their friends obey Allâh and go on His Straight Path. Or, are one's friends of the type that leads to misguidance, failure and loss?

We should also mention that there are two purposes to meet with friends and companions:

1. Spending the time and having company, and this type's harm outweighs its benefit. The least one could say about associating with this type is that they busy the heart and waste precious time.

2. Associating with those who help one another in piety, truth and patience. Indeed, this type is a prized, precious gain that carries tremendous benefits. However, three types of setback might scale down the benefit one gains from associating with this type: luring each other to say and do improper things, too much association and excessive talking, and this association becoming a habit that gradually brings comfort, but not the religious benefits it started with. Surely, friendship helps either the inner-self that commands evil or the heart and soul that are content (with Faith), and the benefit or fruit this type of association brings forth, if any, are tied to its type. As for good souls, they receive encouragement from the angel, while evil souls are enticed by the devil. Allâh, with His Eternal Wisdom, has made the good (husbands, persons, statements) for the good (wives, persons, statements) and the opposite for the opposite.[1]

---

[1] *Al-Fawâ'id*, by Imam Ibn Al-Qayyim, p. 68

Imam Abu Hatim said:

> "The honorable person becomes soft if he is begged, while the evil one becomes harsher if he is treated with leniency. Moreover, the generous (or honorable) person honors honorable people and neither insults the wicked nor harms the wise nor jokes with fools nor associates with sinners. The honorable person prefers his brethren to himself and gives them from what he owns; if a brother of his had a wish, he strives hard to fulfill it; if he found affection from a friend, he does not give thought to enmity; and to he who offers sincere friendship and brotherhood, he does not decline any request from him."[1]

Sincere and righteous friends help each other in this life and in the Hereafter, for their friendship is pure and their brotherhood is true, and thus, it is befitting that their relation continues on to the Last Life. Muhammad bin Yusuf Al-Asfahani said:

> "Who is like the righteous friend? Your family would be dividing the inheritance you left behind and enjoying your money, while your friend would be sad, concerned about the legacy of deeds you performed and the final destination you will end up in, invoking Allâh for you in the darkness of the night, while you are buried under the sand."[2]

Another aspect of having righteous friends, is that they remain dedicated to the memory of their deceased friends, give away charity on their behalf and invoke Allâh for

---

1 *Raudhat Al-'Uqalâ'*, p. 173

2 *Shathrat Al-Thahab*, vol. 1, p. 97

them to endow them with His Mercy, Favor and Forgiveness.

Furthermore, the example of the friend to his friend is like that of the two hands, they wash each other. Friends cooperate in leading and directing each other to righteousness, share good times as well as bad times and help each other in piety through the journey from the life of the world to the Hereafter. Yet, if one is unable to find a righteous friend and a brother in Allâh, then loneliness, reciting the Qur'ân and reading beneficial books are better for him or her than having evil and wicked persons for friends.

Malik bin Dinar said:

> "Avoid every companion who does not bring a righteous benefit to you."[1]

Moreover, Bakr bin Muhammad Al-'Abid said:

> "Dâwud At-Ta'i said to me: 'O Bakr! Be cautious with people, as you are cautious of beasts of prey.'"[2]

Furthermore, Abdul-Aziz bin Al-Khattab said:

> "A huge black dog stood next to Malik bin Dinar and he was told, 'O Abu Yahya! There is a dog standing next to you.' He said, 'Better than having a wicked man for a companion.'"[3]

When 'Ali bin Al-Husain visited Muhammad bin Usamah bin Zaid, who was gravely ill at the time, Muhammad started crying. 'Ali asked him why he cried, Muhammad

---

1 *Hilyatul-Auliyâ'*, vol. 2, p. 372

2 *Raudhatu Al-'Uqalaa'*, p. 82

3 *Raudhatu Al-'Uqalâ'*, p. 82

bin Usamah replied:

> "'Because I have a debt.' 'Ali asked how much the debt was and Muhammad replied, 'Fifteen thousand dinars.' 'Ali said, 'Then, your debt is my debt.'"[1]

Describing various types of friendship and companionship, Ash-Sha'bi said:

> "Honorable people are the fastest to offer their friendship and the slowest in turning towards enmity. Their example is the example of a silver cup: it does not shatter easily and is mended with ease. In contrast, wicked people are the slowest to offer friendship and the fastest to turn enemies. They are like a clay cup, easy to break but hard to mend."

Moreover, Imam Abu Hatim said:

> "The honorable person appreciates whoever favors him, gives excuse when his friends decline to help him, keeps ties with those who sever them, draws closer to whoever keeps relation with him, grants and favors those who seek his help, and feels pity and kindness for whoever he thinks is weak. As for those who mistakenly perceive him as being weak, death would be dearer to them than the consequences of their error.[2] As for the wicked, his are the opposite of these qualities."[3]

---

1 *Hilyatu Al-Auliyâ'*, vol. 3, p. 141

2 Its means honorable persons are not weak and able to defend themselves sufficiently. Those who see weakness in the forbearing and calmness of honorable persons will thus regret it if they seek to exploit this perceived weakness, for the response will be fierce and swift.

3 *Raudhatu Al-'Uqalaa'*, p. 174

A wise man once advised his friend:

> "Goodness is encompassed by three qualities: if you do not spend your day in what is an asset for you, then do not spend it in what is against you; if you do not have righteous friends, then at least do not associate with the wicked; and if you do not spend your money in Allâh's Pleasure, then beware of spending it in what brings about His displeasure."[1]

Abdullah bin Al-Walid said:

> "Abu Ja'far Muhammad bin 'Ali asked us, 'Does any of you insert his hand in his brother's pocket and take whatever he wishes?'[2] We said, 'No.' He said, 'Then you are not brethren as you claim!'"[3]

A wise man gave this advice:

> "Only befriend those who will keep your secret, cover your errors, help you in times of hardship, prefer and favor you in times of comfort, spread your qualities and forgo your mistakes.[4] If you find none having these

---

1 *Az-Zuhd*, by Al-Bayhaqi, p. 310

2 Thus feeling so strongly and deeply about brotherhood that one knows what he has is for his brethren and what they have is his. This way, one will take from his brother's pocket knowing that his brother would never object, and he allows his brother to take whatever he wants from his pocket without objection. One time, a man visited his friend and found that he was not at home, and at the door he found a beggar. He told the servant of his friend to bring some money from inside and gave it to the beggar. When his friend returned and found out what happened, he said to his friend, 'Thank you for keeping good relation with me; for you brought me Allâh's reward while I was away.'

3 *Hilyatul-Auliyâ'*, vol. 3, p. 187

4 Of course, one always advises his brethren and strives hard to make

qualities, then befriend your own self."

Moreover, Imam Abu Hatim said:

> "The wise person should seek refuge with Allâh from the companionship of he who neither offers encouragement when one remembers Allâh nor reminds (of Allâh, one's Islamic duties and obligations, and so forth) if one forgets; this type would lure one to abandon Allâh's *Dhikr* (praising, appreciating, thanking, invoking and supplicating to Allâh) altogether if he or she forgets Allâh's remembrance. Verily he whose company is wicked is the worst one among that company, and just as the righteous person prefers the company of the righteous, the wicked accompanies the wicked."[1]

When one is living during difficult times and suffering from hardships, his faithful righteous friend will distinguish himself from others by offering sincere advice and comfort to his aggrieved friend, thus, lessening the effect of the hardship he suffered and the burden he carried. However, when times are easy and life is smiling for one, he will find an abundant supply of friends and companions.

To continue about another aspect of friendship, we should assert that in this life, death is the hardest of hardships, and therefore, we should think about the effect of one's death on his or her friends and companions. For instance, are one's friends of the type that when one is laid in the grave, they would forget him and stop mentioning his name (by witnessing the attitude and conduct of these friends with

---

himself and them as righteous as they could be to receive Allâh's pleasure and rewards.

1 *Raudhat Al-'Uqalâ'*, p. 102

regards to a friend that they had already lost to death), In this case, would the deceased person's children fall victim to poverty, need, loss, in addition to, becoming orphans?[1]

Our *Salaf* used to keep in touch, inquire about and fulfill the needs of their deceased friend's children for several years after he died![2] It is for this reason that 'Umar رضـى الله عنه offered this beneficial advice:

> "Befriend sincere brothers and you will comfortably live in their midst. Verily, they are a delight to look at in easy times and a provision to turn to in difficult times."

Always think good of what your friend does, unless you hear of something definite about his conduct that would compel you to part with him. Beware of your enemy and be cautious with your friends, except the faithful and truthful among them and certainly, only those who fear Allâh are faithful and truthful to their friends.

Do not befriend the wicked, because you might learn from their wickedness, and never expose your secrets to this type of people.[3]

Moreover, Malik bin Dinar said:

> "It is better for you to transport rocks for the righteous than to eat sweets with the wicked."[4]

Further, Abu Hatim said:

---

1 again, by taking lessons from experience with regards to the degree of faithfulness these friends had to a deceased friend and if they offered any help to his family and children

2 *Minhaju Al-Qasidin*, p. 108

3 *Minhaju Al-Qasidin*, p. 108

4 *Raudhat Al-Uqalaa'*, p. 100

> "The wise person neither stains his own honor nor teaches himself the ways and means of evil by accompanying the wicked. Rather, the wise strives to protect his honor and better his own self by associating with the righteous. Ultimately, experience exposes the true reality of all people as compared to what their outward appearance suggests."

Sometimes, Abu Hanifah would sit to a man he passed by without a reason or prior acquaintance with him. When he left, he would ask the people if that man had a need, so that he could fulfill it for him, and would visit him if he fell ill. This tremendous generosity and kindness would encourage that man to befriend Abu Hanifah thereafter.[1]

As we mentioned, there are rights and obligations that come with friendship. For instance, Sa'id bin Al-'Aas said:

> "My friend has three rights on me: if he draws closer I welcome his closeness, if he talks I listen and if he wishes to sit I make room for him."[2]

Allâh mentioned some of these rights and responsibilities when He described the believer's conduct and mannerism towards each other:

﴿رُحَمَآءُ بَيْنَهُمْ﴾ [الفتح: ٢٩]

"Merciful among themselves."

The exalted level of mercy the believers have for each other becomes perfect when one does not fully enjoy delightful foods or happy occasions if his brethren are not sharing these delights or occasions with him. Rather, one misses his friends in this case and feels alone in their

---

1 *Tarikhu Baghdad*, vol. 13, p. 360

2 *Al-Ihyâ'*, vol. 2, p. 191

absence.[1]

The Messenger of Allâh ﷺ said:

«خيرُ الأَصْحَابِ عِندَ الله خَيرُهم لِصَاحِبه».

"The best companions with Allâh are those who are the best to their companions." (*Ahmad* and *At-Tirmidhi* and rendered authentic by Al-Albani)

These are the benefits of associating with righteous people, who help you in times of need and remind you when you err. They help you in righteousness and piety and recommend patience to you. Therefore, befriend pious people and be neighborly to the righteous. In comparison, the other type of company, the wicked and the sinners, offer this: lures to commit sin, encouragement of ignoring acts of obedience and direction to committing prohibitions. Knowing this type does not help one in this life and only leads to misery and sorrow in the Hereafter. Allâh has described companions of this type as being enemies to each other on the Day of Resurrection, thus putting a disastrous end to this evil association and friendship:

﴿ٱلْأَخِلَّآءُ يَوْمَئِذٍۭ بَعْضُهُمْ لِبَعْضٍ عَدُوٌّ إِلَّا ٱلْمُتَّقِينَ﴾ [الزخرف: ٦٧]

"Friends on that Day will be foes one to another except *Al-Muttaqûn* (the pious)." (43:67)

Abu Ad-Dardâ' رضي الله عنه used to often visit the graveyard and comment when asked:

"I sit with people who remind me of the Hereafter and do not backbite me when I am absent!"[2]

We should also mention that the *Salaf* used to choose as

---

1 *Al-Ihyâ'*, vol. 2, p. 191

2 *Minhaju Al-Qasidin*, p. 432

friends, old, religious, wise and forbearing people whose hair had become white and who gained wisdom, experience and respect through the years. Abu Amr bin Al-'Alâ' said:

> "Sa'id bin Jubair saw me associating with some young men and he asked, 'Why do you associate with young people? Associate with old people instead.'"[1]

Surely, those who get used to associating with old, righteous people will not feel satisfaction if they associate with young men instead. This is because they listen to words of wisdom coming from old people, wisdom they earned through years and decades of experience. Also as compared to young people, old, righteous people often remember Allâh in *Dhikr*, invoke Him for forgiveness and praise and appreciate Him for His Favors and Bounties.

Otherwise, one should follow the advice of Abu Ad-Dardâ':

> "A righteous companion is better than loneliness and loneliness is better than a wicked companion. Further, he who directs to righteousness is better than he who is idle, but he who is idle is better than he who directs to evil."

Moreover, Abu Hatim said:

> "The wise person does not associate with the sinners, because association with them is a piece of the Fire. In contrast, four traits bring happiness and comfort: having an agreeable wife, righteous offspring, pious brethren and friends, and sufficient provisions in one's own homeland. Moreover, it is a fact that those who associate with the wicked and sinners are never safe from their harm and gain a stained reputation

---

1 *Raudhat Al-Uqalaa'*, p. 101

among people."

Az-Zuhri once asked:

"What benefit does the wicked bring about?"[1]

Wahb bin Munbih described 'association with the fools', when he said:

"The fool is just like a worn out garment: if you mend it from one side it gets torn from another, and just like broken clay: it can neither be brought back together, nor made into clay again."

Association with fools brings various types of hardships and difficulties. They wake you tiresome; they curse you if you avoid them. If they give you something, they keep reminding you of the favor; if they take you into confidence, they suspect you would expose their secrets; if you say a secret to one of them, he exposes it; if they are above you socially, they look down at you; but if they are below you socially, they defame you.[2]

Does this description befit much of what today's companionships are about? Therefore, dear Muslim, what is the benefit of associating with the sinners, wicked, fools and evildoers? Certainly, this type of friendship is bound to produce separation, enmity, loss and destruction. One Day, the affection this friendship pretends to bring, will vanish and so will the love, because it was built on the tip of a deep hole in the Fire.

'Ali bin Al-Husain said:

"No two persons accompany each other in sin, but

---

[1] *Raudhat Al-Uqalâ'*, p. 65

[2] *Raudhat Al-Uqalâ'*, p. 122

will soon separate from each other in sin."[1]

This is because sin is a bond and weak as the house of a spider; it is easily torn. The ties and relations that this type of friendship represents are false and superficial, for they were establishing around sin and mutual material benefit, and when these objectives met, this friendship ends as well. In contrast, the strongest friendship is that built around brotherly love for Allâh Alone, bringing together friends who remind each other of Allâh if they forget, and alert each other if they err, all the while seeking Allâh's reward in the affection and pure brotherly love they have for each other. Surely, a friend who reminds you of Allâh's rights on you and helps you perform acts of worship is the best brother, companion and friend you could ever have. This type of friend is better for you than those who might help you financially or favor you with a material possession. Bilal bin Sa'd said:

> "A brother of yours who, whenever he meets you, reminds you of your share with Allâh,[2] is better than a friend who places a dinner in your hand every time he sees you."[3]

The righteous type of companion directs you to the path of the Hereafter, helps you take sufficient provision for it from this life, makes the path of worship and obedience easy for you and opens the doors to piety before you. This type, is the type that fears Allâh, remembers His Perfect Watch,

---

1 *Al-Bidayah wan-Nihayah*, vol. 9, p. 121

2 Its reminds you of Allâh's rights and your excellence or inadequacy in fulfilling them, thus, reminding you of your share of Allâh's rewards according to the degree of obedience you submit to Him.

3 *Hilyatu Al-Auliyâ'*, vol. 5, p. 225

feels fright of Him and questions them concerning their own errors and mistakes.

Abdullah bin ‘Umar رضـــى الله عـــنهما commented on the importance of loving righteous Muslims for Allâh’s sake and associating with them:

> “By Allâh if I fasted all days, stood in prayer all nights and spent all of my money in Allâh’s cause, yet, I died while disliking those who obey Allâh and liking those who disobey Him, my righteous acts will not avail me in the least.”[1]

Righteous friends also give good, beneficial advice. Muhammad bin Yunus bin Musa narrated that a man asked Zuhair bin Na‘im: “What advice do you suggest for me, O Abu Abdur-Rahman?” Zuhair replied:

> “Beware that Allâh takes you away while you are engaged in heedlessness.”

Furthermore, it is a fact that the righteous treats people kindly and mercifully. For instance, Yazid bin Abu Habib said:

> “I will not let a brother of mine be angry with me twice in a row. Rather, I will remove what made him angry the first time.”[2]

---

1 *Al-Ihyâ’*, vol. 2, p. 175

2 *Tathkiratu Al-Huffath*, vol. 1, p. 130

An excellent friendship, brotherhood and companionship!

Another aspect of befriending righteous people is explained by this example. Several of Al-Hasan's friends went to visit him and found that he was asleep, so they started eating from the fruits Al-Hasan had in his house. When he woke up, Al-Hasan commented:

> "May Allâh grant you His Mercy! This, by Allâh, is what brothers do (at the houses of their brethren and true friends, and they too will allow their friends and brethren to do the same in their own houses)."[1]

Moreover, Fath Al-Mausili visited a friend of his who was absent and asked his family to bring out the box where he kept his money and took what he wanted from it. When his friend came back, his servant told him what happened. He said, feeling elated and happy:

> "If you are saying the truth, then you are free in Allâh's cause."[2]

To continue, Al-'Auza'î wrote to one of his friends:

> "Know that you have been cornered from every direction (facing various dangers of life, each having the potential of ending your life) and are being led further on the journey (to the Last Life) each day and night that pass. Therefore, beware of Allâh and your stand before Him tomorrow, beware that Day might be the last Day you meet Him (if you die as a disbeliever and thus end up in Hellfire for eternity).

---

[1] *Minhajul-Qâsidin*, p. 108

[2] *Al-Ihyâ'*, vol. 2, p. 189

Peace be upon you."[1]

Indeed these are the beneficial and faithful friends and companions who offer true love and sincere advice. Therefore, chose this type as friends, as 'Ali رضـى الله عـنه advised you:

> "Befriend righteous people, for they are an asset in this life and the Hereafter. Have you not heard the statement of the people of the Fire:
>
> ﴿ فَمَا لَنَا مِن شَٰفِعِينَ ۝ وَلَا صَدِيقٍ حَمِيمٍ ﴾ [الشعراء: ١٠٠-١٠١]
>
> 'Now we have no intercessors. Nor a close friend (to help us)?'" (26:100-101)

Moreover, righteous company fears the possibility of uttering an evil word for which they would earn a sin. In contrast, today's audiences and meetings have not weighed against the Qur'ân and *Sunnah* so that one knows the righteousness or evilness of the actions and statements that occur in such audiences. Rather, some of them contain words of ridicule against the Qur'ân and *Sunnah*, we seek refuge with Allâh from this evil behavior.

The *Salaf* had an exalted standard concerning choosing whom to take as friends, leaving us a beneficial legacy that provides us with the scales to choose those who deserve our companionship and friendship. For instance, Malik bin Dinar advised Mughirah bin Habib:

> "Every companion and friend from whom you do not earn a religious benefit then discard him and his friendship."[2]

---

1 *Hilyatul-Auliyâ'*, vol. 6 p. 140

2 *Az-Zuhd*, p. 449 and *Sifatus-Safwah*, vol. 3, 286

Therefore, the religion is the true scale with which you could and should weigh all things, people and statements. Otherwise, one will end up with unsuccessful and evil choices. This neither means that you would be able to find error-free friends and companions nor that one should discard his friends if any error occurs by them.

For instance, Shaikh Al-Islam Ibn Taymiyyah said:

> "If every time two Muslims have a dispute they part ways as a consequence, then no affection or brotherhood will remain among Muslims!"[1]

Also, Fudhail bin 'Iyâd said:

> "He who seeks a brother pure of shortcomings will remain brotherless!"[2]

Moreover, Abu Hatim gave this advice:

> "The wise person, whom Allâh has granted the companionship of another Muslim whose friendship is sincere, should hold onto that friend. He should keep relations with this friend even if he severed them, go to him if he went away, give him even if he did not give, draw close to him if he withdrew far away, and in short, act as if he was one of his friend's pillars."[3]

As we stated, one should not think ill of his friends' behavior, but should instead give them excuses for the actions or statements that they might make or utter. For instance, the daughter of Abdullah bin Muti' said to her husband Talhah bin Abdur-Rahman bin 'Auf رضـــى الله عـــنه,

---

1 *Majmu' Al-Fatawa* vol. 24, p. 173

2 *Raudhat Al-Uqalâ'*, p. 169

3 *Raudhat Al-Uqalâ'*, p. 103

who was one of the most generous men of Quraish in his time:

> "I have never seen a worse people than your companions!" He said to her, "Why is that?" her husband asked. She said, "I see that when you are wealthy they associate with you and when you are in need, they abandon you." He replied, "Rather, this is a sign of their good behavior. They come to us when we are able to be generous with them and abandon us when we are unable to fulfill their rights on us."

This is how one gives excuses for his friends and finds the best explanation for however they behave with him. Further, this aspect of friendship that we learned from our *Salaf* indicates their piety, faith and good behavior.

Whenever Abdullah bin Al-Mubarak intended to perform *Hajj*, he would ask his companions and friends:

> "Anyone among you who intends to perform *Hajj* this year, let him bring the money he intends to take with him to me, so that I spend from it on him." He would collect the money they intended to take with them for *Hajj* expenses and wrap each one's money in a cloth, write its owner's name on it and place it in a box. He would accompany them to *Hajj* and spend well on their needs and means of transportation, as well as, being kind to them and easy going. When they would finish the *Hajj* rituals, he would ask them, "Have your families asked you to bring something with you for them?" He would then buy for each one of them the gifts that his family asked him to bring back and when they went back to their city, he would send someone to go before them and ask the families of his companions to clean their

homes and prepare them for their coming. After they returned, he would make a feast and invite them to it, and they would eat and receive the clothes he gave them as gifts. He would then open his box, take out the pieces of cloth and give back each one his money on which he wrote his name. They would take their money and go back to their homes.[1]

Shu'aib bin Harb said:

> "Sit with two types of men: one who teaches you righteousness and one who learns righteousness from you, but run away from the third type."[2]

Therefore, it is time we examine the type of companions and friends we have around us.

To help us give each friend what he deserves of attention and friendship, let us read what Ibn Al-'Jauzi wrote about this subject:

> "I had friends and brethren whom I thought highly of, but experienced some coldness from them, in addition to, ignoring the rights and duties of friendship and brotherhood. Therefore, I started admonishing them. I then said to myself that admonishing does not help, for in this case, these friends will be good for being the subject of blame rather than for friendship. I thought about cutting relations with them, but contemplated that this measure is not suitable either. I realized that there are three types of friends: acquaintances, friends outwardly and brothers inwardly. I then said that it is better to move down

---

1 *Al-Bidayah wan-Nihayah*, vol. 10, p. 203

2 *Sifatus-Safwah*, vol. 3, p. 8

these brothers and friends from the stage of brotherhood to the stage of outward friendship. If they were not suitable for this stage, I would move them farther down to the rank of acquaintances and treat them as such."

Furthermore Yahya bin Mu'adh said:

> "The majority of friends today are merely acquaintances and few among them are true friends.'"

For these reasons, beware of being deceived by those who show you affection. By the passage of time, their relation with you will be exposed in its true reality. You might discover that they have been deceiving you, seeking a certain material gain they wished to earn from associating with you.

Al-Fudhail bin 'Iyâd said:

> "If you want to befriend someone, make him angry and see how he responds. If his response was mannered, you should befriend him! However, in the present time, if you make a 'friend' angry, he will instantly become an enemy!"[1]

If this was the case in their time, how is it then in our time when people have become less kind, and honor has become scarce, except for the few to whom Allâh has granted His Mercy? Once, Abdullah bin Al-Mubarak was on a journey with an ill-mannered man with whom Ibn Al-Mubarak was patient and forbearing. When they parted, Ibn Al-Mubarak cried and replied when asked why he cried:

> "I felt pity for him. We parted ways, but he kept his

---

1 *Saidul Khatir*, p. 497

ill-manners with him!"[1]

Furthermore, Al-Fudhail bin 'Iyâd said:

> "Associate with those who have good behavior, for they will only call you to goodness, and accompanying them provides comfort. As for ill-mannered persons, they only call to evil. Therefore, do not associate with them, so that you save yourself from their ill conduct. I prefer associating with a sinner who has good mannerism, to associating with a worshipper whose mannerism with people is unbecoming. Verily, the former type (the sinner who has good conduct in public) uses caution with people, who like him because he is easy going, while the latter, who has bad mannerism, is despised and disliked to people."[2]

There are signs that indicate one's good mannerism. For instance, Yusuf bin Asbat said:

"There are ten signs of good manners and they are:

> "1. Little arguing. 2. Listening well. 3. Avoiding searching for shortcomings. 4. Covering mistakes. 5. Finding excuse, 6. patience when annoyed. 7. blaming one's own self. 8. Seeing one's own faults rather than other people's faults; 9. Having a beaming face with the young and the old. 10. Saying kind words to those who are below and above one (with regards to religious knowledge, righteousness, social status and so forth)."[3]

---

1 *Al-Ihyâ'*, vol. 10, p. 57

2 *Raudhat Al-'Uqalâ'*, p. 64

3 *Al-Ihyâ'*, vol. 3, p. 77

Allâh's Statement offers a superior description:

﴿ خُذِ ٱلْعَفْوَ وَأْمُرْ بِٱلْعُرْفِ وَأَعْرِضْ عَنِ ٱلْجَٰهِلِينَ ○ وَإِمَّا يَنزَغَنَّكَ مِنَ ٱلشَّيْطَٰنِ نَزْغٌ فَٱسْتَعِذْ بِٱللَّهِ إِنَّهُۥ سَمِيعٌ عَلِيمٌ ﴾ [الأعراف: ١٩٩-٢٠٠]

> "Show forgiveness, enjoin what is good, and turn away from the foolish (i.e., don't punish them). And if an evil whisper comes to you from *Shaitân* (Satan), then seek refuge with Allâh. Verily, He is All-Hearer, All-Knower." (7:199,200)

This *Âyah* gives four rulings and guidelines concerning dealing with other people, and they are: showing forgiveness, enjoining righteousness, turning away from the foolish and seeking refuge with Allâh from the whispers of the devil. Ja'far As-Sadiq was reported to have commented on this *Âyah*:

> "No other *Âyah* in the Qur'ân combines all aspects of good mannerism than this *Âyah*." (*Fath Al-Bari, Sharh Sahih Al-Bukhâri*, 8:306)

Moreover, 'Umar رضي الله عنه reminded us that achieving righteousness is easy and within reach:

> "*Birr* (i.e. good mannerism) is easy to perform: Have a beaming face and speak good words."[1]

Also Mujahid bin Jabr mentioned some of the signs and aspects of good manners and the rights of being brothers in Allâh's cause, when he said:

> "Neither look your friend in the eye excessively, nor ask him where he came from or where he is headed to."[2]

---

1 *Al-Ihyâ'*, vol. 3, 129

2 *Sifatus-Safwah*, vol. 2, p. 209

In contrast many questions of this sort are being raised in today's audiences and meetings. In this context, we could understand why Imam Malik said once:

"I never sat down with a fool!"

Mujahid said, yet explaining another aspect of good mannerism:

> "I accompanied Ibn 'Umar رضى الله عنهما so that I could serve him, but he used to serve me!"[1]

The *Salaf* had these and many other qualities that ensured the continuation of friendship and companionship. This is why we reiterate that the benefit and good effect of the righteous company lasts until the end:

﴿ ٱلْأَخِلَّآءُ يَوْمَئِذٍۭ بَعْضُهُمْ لِبَعْضٍ عَدُوٌّ إِلَّا ٱلْمُتَّقِينَ ﴾ [الزخرف : ٦٧]

> "Friends on that Day will be foes one to another except *Al-Muttaqûn* (the pious)." (43:67)

This fact alone should encourage us to let love in Allâh assume its rightful place with regards to friendship and companionship.

Ahmad bin Harb said:

> "I worshipped Allâh for fifty years, but tasted the delight of worship only after I abandoned three things: I discarded seeking people's pleasure, and thus was able to speak the truth. I abandoned associating with the wicked, and thus tasted the delight of accompanying the righteous. I ignored the delights of this world, and thus tasted the delight of the Hereafter."[2]

---

1 *As-Siyar*, vol. 4, p. 452

2 *As-Siyar*, vol. 11, p. 34

However, when a Muslim does not find the friend who will help him go firmly and righteously on the journey from this life to the Hereafter, then let him be as Ahmad bin Hanbal suggested:

"I find loneliness more comforting in my heart!"[1]

Love in Allâh

Love in Allâh is the strongest tie of Faith and the type of love that lasts and remains. It starts in this life and continues until and throughout the Hereafter, because it is a type of love that is built on Allâh's obedience and takes it purity from Allâh's religion. The Messenger of Allâh ﷺ said:

«الْمَرْءُ مَعَ مَنْ أحبَّ» .

"One will be gathered (on the Day of Resurrection) with those whom he loves." (*Al-Bukhari* and *Muslim*)

Furthermore, righteous company directs to the path of righteousness, since when the Muslim who has Faith in Allâh loves, he loves for Allâh and only hates for Allâh. Thus, the Muslim loves Allâh's obedient slaves and seeks Allâh's Pleasure by feeling love, brotherhood and sincerity for them. The Prophet ﷺ said:

«ثَلاثٌ مَنْ كُنَّ فيه وَجد بِهِنَّ حَلاَوَةَ الإيمَانِ: أَنْ يَكُونَ اللهُ ورَسولُهُ أَحَبَّ إِلَيْهِ مِمَّا سِوَاهُمَا، وأَنْ يُحِبَّ المرءَ لا يُحبُّه إلّا للهِ وَأَنْ يَكْرَهَ أَنْ يَرْجِعَ فِي الْكُفْرِ كَمَا يكْرَهُ أَنْ يُقْذَفَ فِي النَّارِ» .

"Whoever possesses the following three qualities, will taste the sweetness (delight) of faith: the one to whom Allâh and His Messenger ﷺ become dearer

[1] *As-Siyar*, vol. 11, p. 226

> than anything and anyone else, who loves a person and he loves him only for Allâh's sake, and who hates to revert to disbelief as he hates to be thrown into the fire." (*Al-Bukhâri* and *Muslim*)

Love for Allâh's cause is a part of obedience to Him, it does not seek material gains or earthly lusts, it only seeks to earn Allâh's Pleasure, which is the best prize. Moreover, love for Allâh's sake elevates the Muslim to an exalted rank above suspicion, error and earthly goals and lusts.

'Umar bin Hafs said:

> "Umar bin Abdul-Aziz said to me, 'If you hear a word from a Muslim, then do not think evil of its meaning, as long as you could find a good explanation for it.'"[1]

Surely, he who loves people to treat him kindly, should treat them the same way he wishes they would treat him.[2] Moreover, when one thinks of others the same way he thinks of himself, he will realize his own shortcomings and faults and will be compelled to correct them. Bakr bin Muhammad bin Abdullah said:

> "If you witness your brethren being generous and honoring you, then say to yourself, this is a virtue that they have earned. If you see them fall into a shortcoming, then say to yourself, this is due to an error I have committed."[3]

In addition, Abdullah bin Zaid Al-Jarmi said:

> "If a shortcoming (that a brother of yours fell into) reaches you, try hard to find a good explanation for

---

1 *Tarikhu Al-Khulafaa'*, p. 323

2 *Al-Fawaid*, by Imam Ibn Al-Qayyim, p. 194

3 *Sifatu As-Safwah*, vol. 3, p. 248

it. Otherwise, if you do not find a good explanation, say to yourself that may be, my brother has an excuse that I am unaware of."[1]

Another aspect of good companionship is to meet Muslims with a beaming face, smiling towards them and being kind and forbearing. For instance, 'Hammad said that he has never seen a man who is more smiling to his brethren than Ayyub As-Sikhtiyani.[2] They smiled and were merciful with Muslims, for Muslims have an honor and a status that none else among humanity could reach, and they are as Allâh has described them:

﴿رُحَمَآءُ بَيۡنَهُمۡ﴾ [الفتح : ٢٩]

"...merciful among themselves." (48:29)

It was reported that Muhammad bin 'Ali said:

"A neighbor of Abu Hamzah As-Sukkari wanted to sell his house and when he was asked how much he wanted for it, he replied, 'Two thousands for the house and two thousands for giving up being a neighbor of Abu Hamzah.' When Abu Hamzah was told about this, he sent four thousands to his neighbor and said to him, 'Do not sell your house.'"[3]

Another type of righteous companions are those who become happy when their brethren perform acts of worship. For instance, Salih bin Ahmad bin Hanbal said:

"One of our neighbors passed by and we found that he had used Khidab (changed the white hairs on his head and beard with a type of eastern dye that is

---

1 *Sifatu As-Safwah*, vol. 3, p. 248

2 *Tadhkiratul-Hffath*, vol. 1, p. 131

3 *As-Siyar*, vol. 7, p. 387

brownish in color but never black). My father commented, 'When I see a man resurrecting a *Sunnah* act, I feel happy for him.'"[1]

Abu Mu'awiyah Al-Aswad said, describing another aspect of good companionship:

> "My brethren are all better than I am." He was asked, "Why is that, O Abu Mu'awiyah?" He said, "All of them think that I am better than they are, and those who think that I am better than they are, are better than I am."

These types of good behavior and exalted conduct all originate from Islam, which brought the most perfect and beautiful mannerism and exalted code of conduct.

Again, we should remember that this life is full of shortcomings and that friends make mistakes sometimes, either by committing a sin or by erring with their friends and brothers. When a friend of yours commits a sin and insists on it, it is incumbent on you to advise him softly so that he refrains from the sin, returns to correctness and becomes aright and pious again.[2] Soft admonishment using kind words and reminding one of Allâh are all the basis of good advice. Sufyan Ath-Thauri said:

> "I asked Sa'd bin Kudam, 'Do you like that someone gives you a present consisting of your errors?' He said, 'Yes if it is coming from someone who is advising, but not from someone whose purpose is to admonish.'"[3]

---

1 *As-Siyar*, vol. 11, p. 235

2 *Al-Ihyâ'*, vol. 2, p. 217

3 *Hilyatu Al-Auliyâ*, vol. 7, p. 217

When Abu Ad-Dardâ' رضى الله عنه passed by a man who was being admonished by others because he committed a sin, he asked them:

> "If you found this fellow in a well, would you rescue him from it?" They said, "Yes." Abu Ad-Dardâ' رضى الله عنه said, "Then, do not admonish him and praise Allâh that He has saved you from his sin." They asked, "Should we hate him?" He said, "No, hate his sin, and if he abandons it, he again becomes my brother."

Moreover, it was also reported about two brothers from our *Salaf* that one of them abandoned the path of righteousness and his brother asked if he would shun him. He replied:

> "What he needs from me the most, now that he has fallen into sin, is that I take his hand, advise him softly and invoke Allâh that he returns to the way he was before."[1]

To continue, we mention here a good statement by Imam Abu Hatim:

> "The wise person is required to use good conduct with people and to abandon ill manners. Verily, good mannerism dissolves errors, just as the sun dissolves ice, while ill conduct spoils the deeds, just as vinegar spoils honey. One might have many aspects of good mannerism mixed with some ill behavior, but the little ill behavior on his part spoils his otherwise substantial good mannerism."[2]

Good mannerism requires forbearing and graciousness when one has to confront people or is confronted in public.

---

1 *Al-Ihyâ'*, vol. 2. p. 200

2 *Raudhatl-Uqalaa'*, p. 64

Once, when Ali bin Al-Husain entered the mosque, a man cursed him, prompting the people to want to punish him. 'Ali asked them to leave the man alone and said to him:

> "What Allâh has covered from you of my errors is more than what has been uncovered! Is there anything I could help you with?"
>
> That man felt ashamed, and 'Ali gave him a robe he had and a thousand dirhams. (and that man used to describe 'Ali bin Al-Husain, the son of Al-Husain رضى الله عنه the grandson of the Prophet ﷺ, by saying, 'This is a descendant of the Prophets عليهم السلام!)."[1]

Habib Al-Jallab said:

> "I asked Ibn Al-Mubarak, 'What is the best gift that was given to mankind?' He said, 'A wise mind.' I said, 'If one did not have that?' He said, 'Good conduct.' I said, 'And if one did not have that?' He said, 'An advising friend whom he seeks his council.' I asked, 'If one did not have that?' He said, 'Long periods of silence.' I asked, 'If one did not have even that?' He said, 'Then a swift death!'"[2]

Another good indication of the *Salaf*'s mannerism is that when they wanted to advise someone, they would do it in confidence. One of our *Salaf* once said:

> "When someone advises his friend in confidence, it will be an advice, but if he advises him in public, he will have exposed him."

Furthermore, Al-Fudhail bin 'Iyâd said, while explaining the difference between advising and publicly exposing others:

---

1 *Al-Bidayah wan Nihayah*, vol .9, p. 118

2 *As-Siyar*, vol. 8, p. 397

> "The believer advises in confidence, while the wicked exposes and shames."[1]

Abu Ad-Dardâ' رضى الله عنه said:

> "It is better to advise your friend than severing relations with him, for no one can take the place of your friend if you loose him. Be generous and lenient with your friend, and do not allow an envious person to come in between you and him, for in this case, your friend might die tomorrow and you grieve for him. However, how could you grieve for him after he dies, when you have shunned him when he was still alive?"[2]

Yahya bin Mu'adh explains the role a good friend plays in his friend's life:

> "Your brother is he who makes you aware of your errors, and your friend is he who warns you against sinning."

Al-Khalil bin Ahmad, a scholar of the Arabic language, he teaches us the types of people and the benefit we could present to them:

> "Men are of four types. There is a man who knows, but is not aware that he knows; this type is unaware and you need to alert him. There is a man who does not know and knows that he does not know; this type is ignorant and you should teach him. There is a man who knows and knows that he knows; this type is a scholar, so learn from him. There is a man who does not know, but is unaware that he does not know; this

---

1 *Jami' Al-'Uloom wal-'Hikam*, p. 77

2 *Sifatus-Safwah*, vol. 1, 364

type is wicked, so beware of him."[1]

What type of advise could we give to our friends? When a friend of Abu Hanifah advised him by saying, "*Ittaqi* (fear) Allâh!" Abu Hanifah was shaken and changed color. After a long silence, Abu Hanifah said:

> "May Allâh reward you! How needing are people at all times, those who would give them advice like the one you gave."[2]

We should also assert that advice in Islam is given by the old to the young and by the young to the old, as well as, by the scholar to other scholars. Here is an example of the latter type of advice. Ibrahim bin Adham wrote to Sufyan Ath-Thauri:

> "He who knows his goal will spend whatever it takes to earn it. He who sets his sight free (looking at unlawful things, such as gazing at women, etc.), his sorrow will be prolonged. He who has prolonged hopes, then his acts will become evil. He who sets his tongue free, will destroy himself."

And about beneficial advice, Ash-Shâfi'î said:

> "The most precious things are three: generosity, even though one is not wealthy; fearing Allâh when one is alone; and saying a word of advice to those who are hoped or feared (i.e., friends, people of authority, such as kings and tyrants, and so forth)."[3]

It was reported that Urwah bin Az-Zubair advised his

---

[1] *Tathkiratu Al-Huffath*, vol. 3, p. 788

[2] *As-Siyar*, vol 6, p. 400

[3] *Jami' Al-'Uloom wal-'Hikam*, p. 195

children:

> "When you witness a man perform a good deed, know that there are sisters to this good deed with him. When you witness a man commit a sin, then know that he has sisters to this sin with him. Verily, the good deed directs to more of its kind, while the sin directs to more of its kind."[1]

In continuation about friendship and companionship, we should assert that there are times in one's life that he spends in light entertainment with his friends and company. However, there are conditions and guidelines concerning jesting, such as refraining from exaggeration, not using lies to bring laughs to people, and avoiding excessive laughing. Islam does not need jokers and jesters, but needs serious men who should spend their time seeking knowledge, calling to Allâh, participating in *Jihad*, enjoining righteousness and forbidding evil. As for those who often joke and jest, who use lies to bring laughter to their audience, they harm themselves and their religion tremendously.

Those who are eager to imitate the *Sunnah* of the Messenger of Allâh ﷺ, will give little time for jesting, which must never become a habit or a profession. Al-Ahnaf bin Qays said:

> "'Umar bin Abdul-Aziz said to me, 'O Ahnaf! He who jests often, will suffer in respectability; and he to whom joking becomes a habit, will be taken lightly. This is because when one does something often, he will be known by it among people. Furthermore, he who speaks excessively, will err often and his shyness

[1] *Al-Bidayah wan Nihayah*, vol. 9, p. 115

will gradually decrease. He whose shyness decreases, then his fear of Allâh will decrease as well. He whose fear of Allâh decreases, then his heart will die."[1]

Surely, and as 'Umar bin Abdul-Aziz indicated, those who are serious and have fear from Allâh, will not give much time for jesting, joking or excessive talking. Musa bin Isma'il said:

"If I told you that I never saw Hammad bin Salamah laughing, I would not be exaggerating. He was either busy teaching *Hadith*, reading, praising Allâh or praying. These are the types of actions he divided his days by doing."

This statement indicates that our *Salaf* had fear from what will occur to them in the days to come, in the Hereafter, and from the Event that will tremendously shake the body and heart (the Day of Resurrection). Abdullah Abu Ya'la used to often declare:

"Do you laugh, when your shroud may have already been sewn by the tailor?"[2]

Also, one of our righteous *Salaf* once saw a man laugh excessively and asked him:

"Have you tasted death?" He said, "No." He asked again, "Has your scale of good deeds become heavier (than the scale that contains your evil deed)?" He said, "No." The righteous man asked him, "Have you safely passed over the *Sirat*?[3]" The man replied,

---

1 *Tarikh Umar*, by Ibn Al-Jauzi, p. 200

2 *Al-Ihyâ'*, vol. 3, p. 137

3 the bridge over Hell that everyone must pass to safety and Paradise. As for the sinners and disbelievers, they fall from it into Hell, where only the disbelievers will remain for eternity

"No." The righteous man commented, "Why is this excessive laughing and elation then?" That man said, "This is a promise from me to Allâh that I will never laugh like this again." (We mentioned before that it is the *Sunnah* to smile towards people. Also, if one joked, he should never lie or laugh excessively.)

This man woke up from his sleep and gave heed to the warning. What would he say about today's audiences if he hears the excessive laughing and relentless joking of people and the silly distasteful subjects they talk about?

Al-Harith Al-Ghanwi said:

> "Rib'î bin Hirash vowed not to laugh until he knew where he would end up, in Paradise or the Fire."

Al-Harith went on to say:

> "The man who washed Rib'î bin Hirash, after Rib'î died, said to me that Rib'î kept smiling while being washed until he finished washing him."

Moreover, Umar bin Abdul-Aziz asked Isma'il bin Abdullah, "How old are you?" He said, "Sixty years and some months." 'Umar said to him:

> "O Isma'il, beware of jesting."

Al-Fudail bin 'Iyâd said:

> I was told that Talhah bin Musarrif laughed one day and then admonished himself, "Why do you laugh? Only those who pass safely through the horrors (on the Day of Resurrection) and over the *Sirât* laugh." He then said, "I will not laugh until I know what will become of me when the disaster hits (i.e., after death and what will come afterwards on the Day of Resurrection)," and he was never seen laughing until

he died.

Sa'id bin Salim Al-Qaddah said:

> "I heard Abdul-Aziz bin Abu Rawwad advising one of his acquaintances: 'He who does not heed three warnings, will not take a lesson from any other warning: Islam, the Qur'ân and white hair (or old age)."

Therefore, those who witness how fast days end, how quickly they grow old and the suddenness of death, will they feel delight in being given a bounty or hearing a joke in this life? Surely, the matter is serious and the Reckoning to come is severe and swift.

We mentioned how serious our *Salaf* were and the exalted way they conducted their life and religious affairs, but does this mean that we should not smile or joke lightly with people? Adh-Dhahabi gave a comprehensive answer to this question, when he said:

> "Light laughing and jesting, as well as, smiling are better (than excessive seriousness). There are two reasons why some people of knowledge do not laugh or joke at all. They either do this because of shyness and for fear from Allâh, feeling sad for their own shortcomings; this type of seriousness is acceptable. Or this might be due to foolishness, arrogance and pretending with the people and this type is admonished, just as excessive laughing is admonished."

Smiling and meeting people with a beaming face are types of actions that the Prophet ﷺ legislated, encouraged and practised. For instance, the Prophet ﷺ said:

«تَبَسُّمُكَ في وجْهِ أخيكَ صدَقَةٌ».

"Your smiling at your brother is a *Sadaqah* (an act of charity)." (*Al-Bukhâri*, *At-Tirmidhi* and *Ibn Hibban*; this *Hadith* was rendered authentic by Al-Albani)

In addition, Jarir رضى الله عنه said:

"Whenever the Messenger of Allâh ﷺ saw me, he smiled." (*Al-Bukhâri* and *Muslim*)

Further, the Messenger of Allâh ﷺ reported to have said:

«لن تَسَعُوا النَّاسَ بِأَمْوالِكُمْ، فلْيَسَعْهُم مِنكُم بَسْطُ الوَجْهِ».

"You will not be able to accommodate all people with your money (i.e., earn their affection and friendship, help them, etc.) so accommodate them by meeting them with a beaming face." (*Al-Hakim*, *Al-Bazzar* and Abu Ya'la, but this *Hadith* has weakness in its chain of narration).

In summary, Muslims should always avoid excessive laughing, talking, jesting and joking, so that they do not contradict the *Sunnah* or to be taken lightly by people. Further, those who are always serious, should smile and have a beaming face, because this is the *Sunnah* that the Prophet ﷺ legislated in statement and practice. In Islam, every type of excessiveness is rejected, and one has to strive hard to correct and restrain himself.[1]

We should assert that even though having a good company of true friends helps one perform the acts of worship, strengthens his religious resolve and encourages his heart, a Muslim still needs time to be by himself so that he weighs and analyzes his deeds and actions, just as 'Umar رضى الله عنه stated:

---

[1] *As-Siyar*, vol. 10, p. 140

"Take a good share of aloneness."[1]

We do not mean here to abandon associating with people all together or ignoring their rights that the religion has given them, but to take some time alone. Furthermore, those who are tested by having evil companionship will benefit from having time alone, might that Allâh helps them shun their evil friends and associates, as is evident by this advice from 'Umar رضى الله عنه:

"Being alone saves one from evil associations."[2]

Also Abu Dhar رضى الله عنه said:

> "The friend who directs to righteousness is better than the friend who is idle, while the friend who is idle is better than the friend who directs to evil."[3]

Therefore, having a friend who is idle is better than associating with the wicked, and being alone is just as good as having a friend who is idle and silent. To further indicate the virtue of aloneness (sometimes), Masruq stated:

> "One ought to have some time alone so that he reminds himself of his errors and seeks Allâh's forgiveness for them."[4]

This type of aloneness (done periodically) carries several benefits, especially if it keeps one away from wicked companionship that indulges in backbiting and spreading calumnies and malice. Isma'il bin Muhammad said:

---

1 *Al-'Uzlah*, p. 18

2 *Al-'Uzlah*, p. 18

3 *Al-'Uzlah*, p. 57

4 *Al-'Uzlah*, p. 39

> "I heard Ibn Ibrahim say, 'If being alone sometimes does not help except in keeping you away from those who indulge in backbiting, it will be worth it.'"[1]

Many among us do not like to be alone and cannot remain away from people. A wise man once said that this kind does like aloneness:

> "Because they are empty of virtues and do not have righteousness in them. This is why this type repels aloneness by associating with people excessively. If their inner-selves had goodness in them, they would want to be alone sometimes so that they contemplate and search for wisdom."

To continue, we ought to know that the Qur'ân, (the Book of Allâh) that contains His Speech, is the best companion to take during the time a Muslim is alone. The Qur'ân brings comfort, delight and healing to sincere Muslims, those who recite and contemplate its magnificent *Âyat* and glorious Verses. Further, it is an evil sign that one feels depressed when he has only the Book of Allâh before him for companion. Also one should spend time to read and comprehend the second revelation that the Prophet ﷺ was given, the *Sunnah*, that consists of his statements, practices, commands and all that he legislated for Muslims.

When Ibn Al-Mubarak was asked, "Why do you not sit with us after we finish the prayer?" he replied:

> "I sit with the companions and the *Tabi'in* (the second generation of Islam), reading their books and following their narrations. Why should I sit with you,

---

[1] *Al-'Uzlah*, p. 31

you backbite people?"[1]

Therefore, one should also read about the understanding of the Companions concerning the way they conducted, comprehended and conveyed the religion. The Muslim *Ummah* is required to follow the Qur'ân, the *Sunnah* and the understanding of the Companions; and righteous group that will be saved from Allâh's torment in Hellfire.

---

[1] *As-Siyar*, vol. 8, p. 398

Several Reminders about the Subject of this Book

1 -- Shabib bin Shaibah said:

> "Some of my brethren visit me once a year, yet they are the friends whom I consider a reserve for this life and after death. Some friends visit me every day, and I might kiss them and they kiss me (on the cheek) in greeting. However, if I could bite them instead of kissing, I would surely do that."[1]

Certainly, one sometimes feels confused due to seeing bad examples for friends and associates everywhere he or she looks!

2 -- Ash-Shâf'î said to Yunus bin Abdul-A'la,

> "O Abu Musa, know that pleasing all people is an unattainable goal and that there is no way to be completely safe from them. Therefore, see where your righteous benefit lies, and adhere by it; and leave people and all that they indulge in."[2]

3 -- We should also remember that Sufyan Ath-Thauri adviced us:

> "One's having many friends is indicative of the weakness in his religion."

To explain Sufyan's statement, Abu Sulaiman said that it means:

> "Had this man not compromised with his many

---

[1] *Al-'Uzlah*, p. 45

[2] *Al-'Uzlah*, p. 79

friends and gave them respect, they would not have increased in number in this suspicious manner. Surely, had he been strong in his religion, he will only befriend those who are pious and righteous, and there are few people from this type."[1]

4 -- Imam Malik said:

> "People are of various types, just like birds. Pigeons go with pigeons and kites associate with kites, ducks with ducks and small birds with small birds. Similarly, every man associates with his kind."[2]

5 -- Finally, here is a comprehensive advice that we collected from the statements of various wise men with regards companionship and friendship.

If you seek ideal friendship, then meet your friends and your enemies with a beaming face, feeling neither humility nor fear from them. Rather, respect those who deserve it without arrogance or excessiveness, and be humble with them without disgrace. Take the middle, best way in all your matters with them, for excessiveness is always criticized and rejected. Do not keep looking back or looking around when you are walking or talking to your friends, nor stand close to a group of men sitting. Rather, you should sit down with them or go on your way after saying the Islamic greeting, *As-Salâmu Alaikum Wa Rahmatullâhi Wa Barakâtuh* (peace be upon you and also Allâh's Mercy and Blessings). When you sit down, be alert and neither cross your fingers, play with your beard or ring, clean your teeth with your fingers, spit, swat at flies, nor yawn in people's faces or while praying. Let your time

---

[1] *Al-'Uzlah*, p. 44

[2] *Raudhatl-'Uqalaa'*, p. 109

spent sitting with them be calm and your speech to them organized. Listen to good words without excessively feeling amazement about them, and do not ask those who uttered these words to repeat them. In case a dispute arises between you and some of your friends, be graceful, do not act hastily and only speak when you are not angry.

When you attend audience, greet them with the '*Salam*', and do not cut across the lines and sit where you find space. This way, you will be closer to humbleness and grace and people would like to befriend you because of your good manners.

Do not associate with the foolish, but if you have to, do not indulge in their speech, backbiting, evil words, or associate with them excessively. Do not joke with graceful people or with the foolish, for if you do, the graceful person will despise you, while the foolish will belittle you. Surely, joking lessens one's grace and is distasteful to the pious. Also, excessive joking brings death to the heart, takes one away from the Lord, directs to heedlessness and disgrace, having empty hearts and thoughts, and exposes one's shortcomings and faults. Pious men said:

> "Joking occurs because of foolishness or arrogance. If one inadvertently sits in an audience where there is joking and excessive talking, he should remember Allâh upon leaving that audience. The Prophet ﷺ said:
>
> «مَنْ جَلَسَ فِي مَجْلِسٍ فَكَثُرَ فِيهِ لَغَطُهُ فَقَالَ قَبْلَ أَنْ يَقُومَ مِنْ مَجْلِسِهِ ذٰلِكَ: سُبْحَانَكَ اللَّهُمَّ وَبِحَمْدِكَ أَشْهَدُ أَنْ لَا إِلٰهَ إِلَّا أَنْتَ أَسْتَغْفِرُكَ وَأَتُوبُ إِلَيْكَ. إِلَّا غُفِرَ لَهُ مَا كَانَ فِي مَجْلِسِهِ ذٰلِكَ».
>
> "He who sits in a gathering where excessive talking occurs and says, before he leaves that audience, '*Sub hanaka Allâhumma wa bihamdika, ashhadu an Lâ*

ilâha illa Anta, astaghfiruka wa atubu ilaik (all praise is due to you, O Allâh, and all thanks. I bear witness that there is no deity worthy of worship except You, I seek Your forgiveness and repent to you), but will be forgiven whatever he did during that audience.'" (*At-Tirmidhi*, *Ahmad*, *Ibn Hibban*)

We should also remember, before we end this book, the greatest friendship that occurred between two persons. Abu Bakr As-Siddiq رضى الله عنه was the best Companion, brother and friend the Prophet ﷺ ever had. Abu Bakr رضى الله عنه helped the Prophet ﷺ in conducting his *Da'wah* throughout the Prophet's Prophethood, during *Hijrah* from Makkah to Al-Madinah and during *Jihad* afterwards, until the Prophet ﷺ died while pleased with Abu Bakr رضى الله عنه. He supported the Prophet ﷺ with his own self, wealth and family for the benefit of the Prophet ﷺ and Islam. This is why the Messenger of Allâh ﷺ said:

«مَا نَفَعَنِي مَالٌ قَطُّ كَمَالِ أَبِي بَكْرٍ».

"No man's wealth ever helped me more than Abu Bakr's wealth." (*Al-Bukhâri* and *Ahmad*)

The Messenger of Allâh ﷺ said:

«إِنَّ أَمَنَّ النَّاسِ عَلَيَّ فِي صُحْبَتِهِ وَمَالِهِ أَبُو بَكْرٍ».

"Among all people, the one who had the most favor on me in his friendship and wealth is Abu Bakr." (*Al-Bukhâri* and *Ahmad*)

We ask Allâh to make us, and you, among those who love each other for Allâh's sake, and may He gather us and you, and our parents, children, wives and relatives in the Garden of Eden. *Âmeen*.